Dear Jack

Life Lessons from a Brain Tumor
Patient to His Two Year Old Son

Nathan C. Sexton

WESTBOW
PRESS®
A DIVISION OF THOMAS NELSON
& ZONDERVAN

WestBow Press books may be ordered through booksellers or by contacting:

WestBow Press
A Division of Thomas Nelson & Zondervan
1663 Liberty Drive
Bloomington, IN 47403
www.westbowpress.com
1 (866) 928-1240

ISBN: 978-1-5127-5920-4 (sc)
ISBN: 978-1-5127-5921-1 (hc)
ISBN: 978-1-5127-5919-8 (e)

Library of Congress Control Number: 2016916598

Print information available on the last page.

WestBow Press rev. date: 10/11/2016

Contents

Introduction

Dear Jack,

This book is written for you, but I hope others can benefit from the new perspective I have on life. I can't express in words how much I love you. You are only two years old as of this writing, and I couldn't be more proud of you.

As I will explain in this book, I have a cancerous brain tumor. I am not sure what the future holds for me, but I would be a bad dad if I didn't attempt to teach you the lessons I have learned through my battle with brain cancer.

If you get anything from this book at all, I want it to be to put your relationship with God and family before anything else. Drive and ambition are both good, but when left unchecked, they can spiral out of control. Our strengths can become our biggest weaknesses, and I want you to avoid the major pitfalls associated with misplaced priorities. Use the life lessons I will teach you in this book to find your own unique way to serve God.

If God decides to call me home early, just know I will be looking down on you from a heaven that is real. A heaven that is full of love and joy. This earthly life is like a grain of sand on a beach when compared to eternal life, and we will reunite back in heaven one day.

For now though, love God, love other people, and make disciples, because that is what we are called to do on earth.

Love,
Dad

1

Growing Up

God made me fast. And when I
run, I feel His pleasure.
—Eric Liddell, *Chariots of Fire* (1981)

As a little background, I grew up in a typical middle-class
American family. My dad, who you call Pops, owned a flooring
business, and my mom, who you call Mussy, was a stay-at-home
mom. I have one older sister, Aunt Hannah, and we had a golden
retriever; we lived in a nice suburban house, and we went to
church every Sunday. I mean, how much more cliché can it get?

I considered myself a Christian because I went to church on
Sundays, was a decent person, and believed that God was real.
Okay, good. So that's done. All the boxes checked. I was always
very active and loved playing sports. I thrived on competition at
an early age, but I could never stick with something long enough
to master it. I became bored and then was on to the next sport. I
am still like that today.

I began working at an early age, something I would encourage you to do. I was fifteen when I began work as a prep chef for a local restaurant that served soups and sandwiches. It wasn't long before I was promoted to "soup chef," and even though I had to come in at five in the morning to get the soups ready for the day, I loved it. To this day, I still keep that job on my résumé.

As a quick side note (being on the employer's side now), I love seeing applicants who start work early and continue working throughout high school and college. To me, it is an important trait to show you can grind it out when things get tough. When you have papers to write but you also have to go to work, it shows employers you can manage your time well.

Music was a big part of my life, and up to this point, it has been for you. Growing up, Pops and Mussy exposed me to all kinds of music, ranging from gospel to seventies funk, jazz, and everything in between. I started playing guitar when I was seven years old, and I played it consistently until I was about eighteen. I also played mandolin in the church band during high school.

You are only two, and I can tell you have the same love of music that I have. You will walk around with a ukulele we got you for Christmas and say, "I want to play guitar like Daddy!" I still pick up the guitar from time to time to play for you.

Jack rocking out on his ukulele!

Out of all the various sports I played as a child, there was one constant I always went back to in my life to find clarity—and still do—and that was running. I remember going on runs with Pops before I could drive. We would have the windows down and listen to Pat Metheny—a contemporary jazz musician—on full blast. I still listen to Pat Metheny when I run just to access those precious memories.

I ran track and cross-country in high school, but I was essentially forced into it. Here is the story of how it went down. Please take this as a lesson, and don't learn the hard way—like I did.

When I turned sixteen, I had the bright idea of taking Pops's brand-new truck while he was out of town; I wanted to go fishing with one of my buddies. It was such a smooth ride that we decided to play the "How fast are we going?" game—a game that entailed me covering up the speedometer and having my friend guess how fast we were going. I know what you are thinking: *Great idea. Great game.* Well, the cop who pulled us over gave us the answer.

"Sir, did you know you were going one hundred miles per hour in a fifty-mile-per-hour speed-limit zone?"

I wanted to say, "Uh, no, because I had the speedometer covered up by my hand and you ruined our game." But I was polite, like my parents had taught me to be if I was ever pulled over. After a lot of yes-sirs and no-sirs, I thought I was getting off the hook. You could tell the cop was kind of easing up. After all, I was a freshly minted sixteen-year-old and just needed a warning.

That didn't happen. He wrote me a massive ticket and ordered me to go to court. I waited to tell Mussy until we arrived at home, and she was extremely upset. She called Pops, and he was flat out angry that I had driven his new truck without permission. As for my friend's mom, she wouldn't let him ride with me for one whole year.

Needless to say, I was up the creek without a paddle. Luckily, we found that paddle when we realized the judge's brother, Steve, was our high school's track and cross-country coach.

Let me take a step back and tell you Steve had wanted me to run for our high school for years. He followed my middle school track "career" when I was younger and knew I had potential. I didn't really play any sports in high school, even though I was a good athlete—mainly because I was so caught up in the social aspects of high school. Steve found his leverage to get me to run, and we found our paddle. Instead of spending hours upon hours of community service and losing my license for a year, he just requested his brother, the judge, make me run track and cross-country for a year.

We took the deal and ran with it. Literally. I ended up being a great sprinter and hurdler. Injuries always kept me from running long distances, but I will get into running form a little later in the book. (And yes, these last few months, I have read various books on running form that have enabled me to run long distances and remain injury free). I hated cross-country because there was too much pain that lasted for way too long. I liked my pain to come in intense, short periods of time. God would eventually change that, though I didn't know it at the time.

2

Strengths and Weaknesses

> The ultimate measure of a man is not
> where he stands in moments of comfort
> and convenience, but where he stands at
> times of challenge and controversy.
> —Martin Luther King Jr.

Pops has always been a hard worker. He sold class rings and cleaned carpets to get through college. When he eventually graduated, his dad—who we called Papaw but who most others called Hotz because of his hot temper—asked Pops to come work for his small paint company. The company performed a variety of tasks, including cleaning carpets, which Pops knew all about.

By this point, Pops and Mussy had Aunt Hannah and me, and Pops traveled a lot while selling class rings. So he decided to take Papaw up on the offer to join the painting company. His first day in the office, he immediately regretted the decision. Let's just say Papaw lived up to his other nickname.

Every now and then, they would get a carpet-cleaning job where the carpet needed to be replaced. Pops started thinking and had the idea of starting a flooring company. Papaw and Pops would be partners, and Sexton Floor Covering was born.

It wasn't too long before Pops turned what was once a little old painting company into a thriving business, and he bought Papaw out. The business continued to grow as his relationships with builders across the region grew—a true rags-to-riches story.

Pops was really involved in our church, Cedar Springs Presbyterian Church, and had been asked by our senior pastor to think about joining the staff. Pops felt a calling to go to seminary and join the Cedar Springs team.

By this time, Sexton Floor Covering was firing on all cylinders. He knew he could sell it for a nice chunk of change, which would allow us to maintain the life we were all used to while he went to seminary and started work at the church.

After praying about it for months, he decided to sell his company. Soon thereafter, Sexton Floor Covering was sold to a company called the Maxim Group, which was traded publicly on the New York Stock Exchange. The deal was done in mostly stock and options. I distinctly remember Pops saying, "If the Maxim Group's stock hits twenty-six dollars a share, we will all go to Hawaii for our next vacation." It was a promising deal, and he felt confident the Maxim Group's stock would continue to go up.

It took him five years to complete seminary, and he graduated summa cum laude (and first in his class). In the fifth year, Maxim Group went completely bankrupt, leaving Pops with a bunch of worthless stock and options. All Pops had worked for his entire life was gone in an instant. I didn't realize it at the time, but this absolutely wrecked him.

I am sure he dealt with some depression; I know I would. Pops and I like to have things mapped out. This was the perfect plan. Sell the business, go to seminary, and join the staff at our church. Why would God do this to our family, right when your pops was trying to serve Him?

He continued on with Cedar Springs, where he started a night service that he preached at. Let me tell you that Pops is a fantastic preacher. The way he can connect with other people through a sermon is truly amazing. He also did some counseling, since he is able to empathize with just about anyone. He is the best person in the world at putting himself in another person's shoes.

To outsiders, everything still looked good. Sure, we had taken a hit as a family, but we were going to get through this.

High school was a great time in my life until it all came crashing down when Pops sat me and your aunt Hannah down at the dinner table while Mussy was taking a bath. He said that he would be going away for a little while because he and Mussy were having some issues.

What? Okay, I know no marriage is perfect, but they would work through it once he had some time to get away and think. I didn't think much of it at the time, because I knew he would come back home. Well, that day never came. I spent countless nights lying beside Mussy while she cried like I had never seen her cry before.

Pops didn't *leave* leave. We still caught up in person and on the phone, but our relationship took a hit. He was the man

I looked up to and admired, and I didn't understand why he was making this decision. It took a while for our relationship to get back to where it was, though I didn't really show it outwardly. Silence is a luxury I took full advantage of. I just went on pretending that everything was normal when, in reality, it was not.

Aunt Hannah was the total opposite. She took it personally. I thought I was being the bigger person by taking the high road and not asking a lot of questions. I felt bad for Pops and thought I needed to comfort him and be there for him. I was trying to manage both sides—Mussy's and Pops's—and ended up not doing either very well.

This all happened when I was a junior in high school. I don't think I realized how much it affected me until now. It wasn't an ugly divorce or anything like that, but divorce is divorce, and it has lasting effects for everyone involved.

Due the decreased income, Mussy had to dust off her résumé and ended up getting a job as a flight attendant, which she is great at and loves! Pops ended up remarrying to a wonderful lady named Debbie; you call her Gimmi. She has been a loving grandmother to you and stepmom to our family.

I tell you this because there is a valuable lesson inside the pain our family went through. Pops's dad, Papaw, could be very generous and kind, but most of the time, he stumbled home inebriated. Pops and his two sisters didn't have a great childhood. Creditors and bill collectors were calling all the time, and at a young age, he was always trying to work deals with them and make excuses for his parents not paying.

Pops wanted to be comfortable and secure (which he associated with money) because while growing up he hadn't had security. Who can really blame him? Isn't that what we all want in life—to feel comfortable and secure? The problem was he let his hardworking tenacity and ambitious ways take over his life in search of this security. Ambition and a hardworking nature are both good in theory, but when left unchecked, they can spiral out of control.

As Pops said recently, "It's not our weaknesses that get us into trouble but our strengths. If our strengths are left uncontrolled, they begin to become false idols." Don't let the gifts God has given us turn into idols.

Pops let comfort and security become his idols, and when Maxim Group went bankrupt and all his security was gone, our family saw the repercussions. Ultimately, it ended up with Mussy and Pops getting a divorce.

Little did I know that the same drive and hardworking tenacity would begin to lead me down the same path, except my brain tumor would stop me dead in my tracks and allow me to rethink my priorities.

———

Mussy, Pops, Aunt Hannah, and Gimmi have all taught me valuable lessons to make me the man I am—or am trying to be—today. Mussy and Pops have been incredible influences on my spiritual life.

Mussy would force me to listen to Tim Keller, the senior pastor at Redeemer Presbyterian in New York City, New York. Despite my teenage resistance to him at the time, I have come to absolutely love him, which you will see by the various Tim Keller references throughout this book. She wouldn't hesitate to tell me the truth if I was out of line. Of course, I never thought I was out of line. I was always trying to justify my actions but would eventually come to see that she was right all along. Mussy holds a very special place in my heart. We have had some difficult conversations since my diagnosis, and I always seem to gain a valuable "nugget" (as she would call it) from each one. She challenges me to become more like Christ on a daily basis.

As a flight attendant, Mussy has had so many great conversations about God with her passengers. People are naturally drawn to her because they notice something is different about her. They notice Christ shining through her, and I have noticed the same. She has inspired me to live a life that is "different"—a life where Christ shines through me. I have a tattoo that quotes Galatians 4:19 that reads, "Until Christ is formed in you". I have adopted it as my mantra and Mussy lives it day in and out. Christ is formed in her.

Since Pops went through seminary and graduated summa cum laude, he knows the Bible inside and out, but he doesn't beat it over your head. He is calculated and wise. He instilled the character in me to make me the man I am today. Character is built by all the small decisions you make during your life—even the small ones. At a young age, I picked up on his constant faith and reliance on God. I remember when I was younger that Pops would come in my room Sunday morning on days when I didn't feel like going to church. He would warm up the socks on my feet (really just rubbing the socks against my feet really fast), which would get me in good enough spirits to get in the car. Pops always knew how to make me laugh.

I would always go to him with any questions. With spirituality, math, girls, or whatever, he would always have the right answer. Given Pops's tough past, he really did everything he could to capture the generosity of Papaw while still managing to be as little like him as possible. No one is perfect; we all sin. Pops is a great, godly man and will be an incredible grandfather to you.

Aunt Hannah is the definition of loyalty. She would do anything for me and not just because she is my sister. She truly loves me. Of course, we had our tiffs growing up, but they were few and far between. We got along well most of the time. She always had a cool boyfriend. When I was younger, I would want to be like whoever she was dating at the time. She would eventually marry an incredible guy, who you call Uncle Moo Cow. His name is Cal Davis, so when you tried to say his name, you were confused and thought his name was Cow. We kind of made you lean in to Moo Cow. She was constantly showing me to new music and introduced me to one of my favorite bands, the Dave Matthews Band.

Gimmi has been amazing to you, despite the fact that we are Tennessee Vols fans and she taught you to say, "Go Bama." As you will see as you get older, she is an incredible host. She always makes sure you have what you need. Sometimes Pops gets a little frustrated because he is thinking, *Let's have a party with paper plates and plastic forks,* but she won't hear of it. She always wants the evening to be special and would rather clean the fine china herself than use paper plates and plastic forks. Let her teach you the ins and outs of a little game called blackjack when you are twenty-one. Somehow, she always walks away with money. She also taught me that a mother's love can come from a stepmom as well.

3

Meeting Your Mom

Simplicity and complexity need each other.
—John Maeda, *The Laws of Simplicity*

Once I graduated high school, I took a much-needed break from running. I had acquired terrible shin splints from constantly running on our high school's track. Being from Knoxville, I followed my high school friends to the University of Tennessee. It honestly never crossed my mind go anywhere else. In retrospect, I wish I had gone away for college, but then I would have never met your incredible, strong mom, Elizabeth. I call her Liz.

Liz and I met sophomore year through a friend of mine, who we called Crabby. Your mom had a day off from rush (she was a Chi Omega), and Crabby and I decided to pick her up and take her to our apartment to hang out. I had seen Liz around campus and thought she was beautiful, so I stepped up my extremely mediocre game when we picked her up. She got into my dark-green Tahoe Z71 (I still regret getting rid of that car), I sang a little Shakira (to get her laughing a little), and we set off to our apartment.

It was a great night filled with laughter. We capped it off with an epic match of Xbox Ping Pong. If my memory serves me correctly, she beat me! At that moment, I knew she was the one for me. Crabby and I took her home, and we said our good-byes. I remember talking to Crabby on the way home about how cool Fogo was. (That was her maiden name and nickname.)

In a couple of days, Pike (the fraternity I was in) and Chi Omega were going to have a mixer (an event where a sorority and fraternity get together), and I was full-on Facebook stalking her. I was trying find something to talk to her about at the upcoming party, and I saw she went on a trip with her family out West to Jackson Hole and Yellowstone.

Okay, so I'd found my ammo. I was going to talk to her about how I had been to Vail and Telluride but never to Jackson Hole or Yellowstone. I had already thought of questions in my mind. *How is Yellowstone? I hear it is beautiful! Was Jackson Hole amazing?*

All I can say is my plan worked. I left with her number. I tried to give her mine, but in classy fashion, she insisted I just call her. Nice move—hook, line, and sinker. I told her I had intramural flag football practice in the morning but would call her immediately after it was over. As I walked home from the mixer, I called one of my best friends, Walter Sheppard, and told him I found the perfect girl.

While I was at my intramural football practice, I collided, head on, with a guy in my fraternity. I came back to the huddle, got the play, and lined up.

"What's the play again?" I asked. They told me the play. Then, before they could even snap the ball, I asked, "Hey, what's the play again?" That's when I stopped remembering.

I was told I was very aggressive and demanded to see "Fogo." Crabby took me to the hospital where I asked him about a thousand times what had happened. I asked him so many times that he wrote out exactly what happened on index cards for me to read for myself. Pops and Gimmi, who met me at the hospital, had no idea who or even what a "Fogo" was. Apparently, I kept saying, "I need Fogo."

Once I finally got back to Mussy's house in Knoxville, I wasn't showing any signs of getting better, but I had my phone. So I called Fogo and explained what had happened. By this time it was late, and I am sure she was thinking, *I shouldn't have given my number to that guy. I knew he wouldn't call.* Then we hung up. I immediately called her back and began explaining what had happened—again. This time Mussy intervened and got on the phone.

"I am so sorry, Elizabeth," Mussy said. "Nathan had a massive concussion and has lost all short-term memory." On the other side of the phone, Liz shot up from her bed, since she had never met or talked to Mussy.

"Mrs. Sexton! I'm Elizabeth. I am so sorry to hear about Nathan. Tell him to get some rest." This is not how I expected Mussy and Liz to meet, but hey, all I can say is it worked out.

———

As your mom and I grew to love each other, we saw how opposite we were. You know the old saying "Opposites attract," but we were completely opposite in almost every way imaginable. She loved funny, romantic comedies. I loved serious, deep dramas. She is very chill—a total type B. I am very high-strung—a total type A. You name it, and we had totally different perspectives on everything, except our faith.

Being total opposites scared us at first, and we had some difficult times navigating various issues. But we came to love the opposite traits in one another. She would help me calm down if I was in one of my crazy, type-A moods, and I would get her up and active if she was in one of her chill, type-B moods.

In short, what made us so different brought us closer. Being opposites made us better people. Isn't that what you want in someone you will be spending the rest of your life with—someone who will not only stick with you in the hard times (Lord knows we have had no lack of hard times lately) but also take you to new heights when times are good? Ultimately, you want to find someone who helps you deepen your relationship with God, through making you a better person inside and out.

———•———

Liz was still finishing up school, and I had just graduated college with a finance degree in 2009, when our country was still coming out of the biggest recession since the great depression. Needless to say, the job market was limited. I had a friend whose dad was pretty high up at Hewlett Packard, and he said they were looking for sales reps for a new facility they opened up in Conway, Arkansas.

I talked to Liz about trying out the long-distance thing, which would give me enough time to decide if I enjoyed being a sales rep. If so, I would have a head start on a career while she finished up school. It was a tough decision, since we had only spent a few weeks apart in the past four years, but we both agreed I should take it.

I couldn't have even pointed Conway out on a map when we started looking for apartments. (It's just north of Little Rock.) I didn't want to move to Conway alone, and HP needed more people. So I recruited one of my good friends, Brian Trautschold—BT as we call him—to come with me. And just like that, we were off to Conway.

As you could imagine, there wasn't much to do in Conway. BT and I joined a gym, where we worked out and played pickup games of basketball. There was a country club not too far from the office so we played a little bit of golf, but outside of that, there wasn't anything to do.

I tried to start running again, since there was a little two-mile loop not far from my apartment, but my left IT band wouldn't let me get past three miles before I was in so much pain I wanted to cry. So I would run two fast miles a couple of times a week. I couldn't pace myself to save my life. Being a sprinter in high school will do that to you. It wasn't long before I just couldn't take the knee pain anymore and decided that humans were not meant to run long distances. Once again, I quit running even though it was something I really enjoyed.

I was miserable in Conway, and so was BT. There is only so much golf and pickup basketball you can play before you will start losing your mind, and I didn't like my job. I hated the fact that I could only talk to your mom on the phone and not see her. Let's just say BT and I weren't in Conway long enough to see four full seasons there. We came to our senses and realized we needed to get out of there.

Your mom had just finished up college, and she is originally from Chattanooga, Tennessee. Chattanooga is one of the best cities in the nation for climbing, and I love to climb. In college, my friends and I used to drive down to Chattanooga just to climb. As a bonus, it is only an hour and a half from my hometown of Knoxville, so we decided to start looking for jobs in Chattanooga.

We both landed jobs pretty quickly: me at a regional bank and your mom at the Chambliss Center for Children. Your mom has an incredible heart for those in need, and this was the perfect job for her. She had performed community service throughout high school and loved it.

Around that time, on a beach trip, I proposed to your mom. Our family goes to the beach every year and since Aunt Hannah is an incredible photographer, we always take family pictures. I secretly planned for her family to be down there at the same time, because she always said she wanted both of our families to be there when I proposed.

We decided to do pictures the first night, mainly because I couldn't wait to propose any longer. We went down on the beach, like usual, for the family photo shoot. After a couple pictures—did I mention I am extremely impatient?—I got down on one knee and immediately asked, "Will you marry me?" I had planned this big, long speech before I was going to ask her, but I couldn't wait a second longer. As soon as she said yes, her family popped out from behind a beach chair rental box (you know those big, white boxes on the beach?), and that was the icing on cake.

We were engaged for about a year until we got married. We had a beautiful wedding the following March at Patten Chapel in Chattanooga.

Your mom and I are leaving the wedding in a confetti shower!

Passion for Work

I used to be afraid of failing at something that
really mattered to me, but now I'm more afraid
of succeeding at things that don't matter.
—Bob Goff, *Love Does*

I wouldn't say banking was my dream job, but I have the same
hardworking tenacity that is in your pops's DNA so I did the best
I could, treating customers who came in the branch with care. For
the most part, I enjoyed it.

Which brings me to another point. It doesn't matter whether
you clean carpets like Pops or are a prep chef for a soup restaurant
like me; always do whatever you do to the best of your ability. In
Tim Keller's book *Every Good Endeavor*, he states, "All work has
dignity because it reflects God's image in us, and also because the
material creation we are called to care for is good."

That quote is packed full of meaning. All work does have
dignity, and you have a certain responsibility to God to make sure

it is done to the best of your ability. The doctor who performed my surgery couldn't have done it without the nurses prepping me. The nurses couldn't have done their job if the janitor hadn't sterilized the operating room. The janitor couldn't have done his job without having cleaning supplies. What I am trying to say is that in God's kingdom, your job doesn't matter. It doesn't matter to God whether you are the surgeon or the person ordering cleaning supplies. What matters is you glorify Him by working hard and loving others, through whatever career path you take.

———•———

While working at the bank, I made a great relationship with Todd Tindall, the wealth-management representative who covered all the high-end clients at our branch. I expressed interest in the wealth-management side of the business, and Todd was quick to pull me onboard.

After about a year, our bank's wealth-management arm was bought out by another firm. I stuck with it for about another year, until I was introduced to someone at yet another wealth-management firm that had a team who needed a junior partner.

After some deliberation, we decided it was the right move, since the bulk of what I would be doing was putting together financial plans for their existing client base. I was probably in the best spot you could be in the financial advising world, but it was so unfulfilling to me. I felt like I had no purpose so I revamped my résumé and began thinking about what I wanted to do.

BT, the friend who braved the pits of Conway with me, had cofounded a company, along with my friends Jared Houghton and Travis Truett, in Chattanooga that was funded by a venture incubator called Lamp Post Group. (Venture incubators provide funding and office resources for equity in the company.) There were a few other companies that Lamp Post was funding so naturally I went to BT to see if any of these startups needed any help.

He mentioned a startup called Bellhops. Bellhops is a tech-enabled platform that connects college students to people needing moving help. Customers go to the website getbellhops.com and book moving help. That information is put on an online dashboard so that student movers, called Bellhops, can pick up jobs around their class schedule—think Uber for moving. To me, Bellhops seemed exciting! Possibly a new adventure and an escape from the wealth-management prison I was stuck in.

I started hanging around the office and getting to know them. It was a small team of four main people. Cam Doody and Stephen Vlahos are the founders, and they quickly hired a COO, Matt Patterson, and CTO, Adam Haney. I got to know Cam the best and he invited me to go mountain biking with him. I had never really been mountain biking before, but who in their right mind would say no to going mountain biking with the cofounder where you are trying to land a job. After about an hour and half of "easy mountain biking," as Cam called it (it was extremely difficult), he informally offered me the position of director of customer experience. The title was a little over the top, because Bellhops, including the leadership team and part-time employees, only had thirteen people. My job would be managing the two part-time employees, who were still students at a local university and worked at Bellhops between classes.

By now I was twenty-seven, and Liz and I had moved into a new house and had you! You were still a newborn, and I was finally starting to make pretty good money, even though I was miserable putting together financial plans every day. I told Liz that if I accepted the job at Bellhops, my salary would be cut roughly in half.

I felt so passionate about this company. I told her I wanted to have a hand in building something great and not just work for a massive corporation or bank. There is not anything wrong with working for a massive corporation or bank, but it wasn't where I was meant to be. Liz said to accept the position. She wanted me to do something I was passionate about and knew I was miserable where I was. We started cutting back wherever we could in order to make our house payments and buy groceries, diapers, and baby food for you.

I went to lunch at a local restaurant with Cam and Matt where they formally offered me the job. I was so excited. But with a lofty title, no management experience, and no true experience in customer service, I was a little nervous. I had big plans to disrupt the whole customer service industry and make it a key element of our business. I was able to build off the customer-first mentality that had already been established by our leadership team.

My first day in the office, Matt Patterson walked me back into our little corner of office space in Lamp Post Group to introduce me to the two guys I would be managing: Ice and BJ. I spent the first week just getting to know them. BJ loved to turkey hunt, and Ice was my go-to guy for new music. I didn't just get to know them the way new managers get to know their subordinates. They were my friends, and I valued their opinions and feedback.

To this day, the culture at Bellhops isn't based on titles, power, or pride. It is based on a love for the person sitting next to you and doing whatever you can to help that person out.

After the first month, I had a good grasp on how the company operated and began to do what I always dreamed of: having a hand in the building of a company. I began reading book after book in my spare time, which was limited due to the long hours at work. The most impactful book I read, during that time, was *Delivering Happiness* by Tony Hsieh.

I highly suggest you read it some day. It discusses Zappos's customer-first culture, and I tried to replicate Zappos's culture in my own way. I created all kinds of customer-first processes, even if, in the beginning, it hurt our business financially because I believed it would help us build a brand that people talked about. I created a massive sign to go in the office that said, "Provide Peace of Mind." That was our department's mission statement—to provide peace of mind to customers, no matter the cost.

I taught myself how to code and perform SQL queries (basically, pulling data) to more efficiently report metrics for my team and save valuable time that needed to be spent elsewhere in the business.

This didn't leave much time for you and Mom. I told Liz, "Just give it a few more years, and I promise it will get easier as we hire more people." She was basically like a single mom for a year and a half. I knew how hard it would be for you all for a few years, but I had convinced myself it would all get better.

It's good to be ambitious and driven, and I would be a bad father if I told you not to be, but always make time for God and your family first. Set aside time to get to know God and build a relationship with Him. Remember what Pops said earlier. "It's not our weaknesses that get us in trouble but our strengths." You will have the same drive and ambition I have. Just don't let it consume you.

5

Growing a Company

> If you personally want to grow as fast
> as your company, you have to give away
> your job every couple months.
> —Molly Graham, chief
> operating officer of Quip

We were forced to grow our department and team at an incredible rate, due to the influx of demand. I get asked a lot about how I was able to scale my team so quickly. It all comes down to hiring great people. Well, how do you know if the people you hire are great?

In the early stages of Bellhops's operations department, it didn't matter what college you went to, or even if you went to college. I wanted people who were so bought into the vision of the company that they would do almost anything for Bellhops. Of course, as you become an actual company, you will need to specialize, but I would worry about that later.

I wanted A players. When Steve Jobs talked about hiring, he talked about only hiring A players because it is a self-policing environment. Think about it. If you are an A player, you are not going to want to work with B players. You want to work with the best of the best. If you hire one B player, then he will bring on a C player to boost his confidence. C players hire D players, and on it goes.

I was completely overworked, and it was time to make my first full-time hire. He was going to be great. He was going to be an A player for sure. At least, I was rooting for him to be an A player because I was in desperate need of one. He was going to take a huge load off my back. Sure, it would take some time to train him, but at the end of the day, it would all be worth it.

Well, it didn't work out. It only took one bad hire for me to see the repercussions it caused. More established companies have training departments created for the sole purpose of training new employees. In a startup, the buck stopped with me. We were about to head into another busy season, and I knew we wouldn't survive without getting some help fast.

We decided to internally promote Jacob Ellis and Zoe Harrison, who are both incredible workers and even better people. We also promoted Amber to run our newly minted concierge team, which consists of hand-holding customers through the moving process. Amber is incredibly driven, efficient, and ambitious. She was the perfect fit for this role and has since taken on more responsibilities.

Then we hired Matt Harb, who had graduated college but was willing to take an eight-dollar-an-hour job as a customer enthusiast. Enthusiasts were the people on the front lines manning the phones. I knew there was something special about Harb the moment I met him. You could tell Bellhops oozed out of his veins before he even started working there. I knew I had found my successor.

With four incredible full-time people performing all the various jobs I had previously done, and with better technology surrounding the platform, I could finally catch my breath. I got a chance to read *High Output Management* by Andy Grove and totally changed my views on management. It's crazy that a book written in the 1980s—before e-mail—is still relevant and impactful today.

Essentially, that book taught me how to be a manager of people, including when to step in and correct someone and when not to. This is an easy concept, but it's hard to put into practice when you are on the line for your coworker's performance. Knowing when to step in is even harder, especially if you are a type-A perfectionist like I am. It was like giving up your baby for someone else to raise.

The best article on this subject I have ever read came from an article that quotes the COO of Quip, Molly Graham.

> "The best metaphor I have for scaling is building one of those huge, complex towers out of Legos," she says. "At first, everyone's excited. Scaling a team is a privilege. Being inside a company that's a rocket ship is really cool. There are so many Legos! You could build anything. At the beginning, as you start to scale, everyone has so many Legos to choose from—they're

doing 10 jobs—and they're all part of building something important."

You have so many choices and things to build during this early phase that it's easy to get overwhelmed. There's too much work—too many Legos. You're not sure you can do it all yourself. Soon, you decide you need help. So you start to add people. That's when something funny happens on a personal level and to teams: People get nervous.

"As you add people, you go through this roller coaster of, 'Wait, is that new person taking my job? What if they don't do it the right way? What if they're better than me at it? What do I do now?'" says Graham. "These are some strong emotions, and even if they're predictable, they can be unnerving." In order to get to a really high-functioning, larger team, you have to help everyone get through this roller coaster. If you don't, you can end up with a real mess."

At this point, we were killing it. Bellhops was growing like crazy, I was now vice president of operations, and we had just raised our series A round of funding. I attempted to give up little pieces of the departments I had built but really struggled to fully trust Harb, Amber, Jacob, and Zoe with my nicely stacked towers of Legos. I feared the day they would remove a Lego and make a change of their own.

Becoming a Leader

Best job I ever had.

—*Fury* (2014)

I was becoming a great leader and pushing Bellhops forward with vigor. Sure, I still had a lot of learning left to do, but my dreams of building up a vital department in a company were coming true.

After watching the movie *Fury*, I was hugely inspired. In fact, I was so inspired I sent out a team-wide e-mail with the subject line: "Fury—the tank that defines leadership." Here is what it said:

> There are many books and movies that attempt to give insight into the inner workings of a fluid, efficient team and what it means to be a leader, but few accomplish that lofty goal as well as the movie *Fury*.
>
> For those who haven't seen it, see it. No ifs, ands, or buts. But in short, *Fury* is set in World War II and

follows a tank crew throughout the final days of the war in Germany. In the fictional story, the tank crew fought and won many battles together and was widely regarded as one of the best tank crews anyone had ever seen. The crew named their tank Fury.

I hesitate to relate war to business, because I know nothing of actual war and would hate to disgrace any true solider, but the metaphor is too good not to dive into.

What made the Fury crew so good? Was it the fact they were all competent in their role? Was it the fact they had a great leader in Don Collier (played by Brad Pitt)? Or was it because their generals gave them good insight and vision into their enemy's movements so that they could be more calculated in their attack?

From here on out, the tank crew will be called the crew. Brad Pitt's character will be called the leader, and the generals will simply be the generals.

It is safe to say not one of the above attributes led to their success as a tank crew, but a combination of all of them, as well as less tangible attributes, such as the culture and attitude.

Early on in the movie, the crew's long-time assistant driver/gunner/friend dies in battle. A typist named Norman, who has never seen a day in battle in his life, replaces him. This was obviously a huge blow for the crew. It would be the equivalent to the Broncos losing a star wide receiver, only to be replaced by a wide receiver who has never played in a football game. So let's look at how the crew responds.

The initial training of Norman is pretty intense, but throughout the whole movie, the leader shows him what it means to be in war and to be a part of the Fury crew. It is not a one-time training session. He is constantly teaching Norman through his own actions, not by telling him to do so. He shows Norman the consequences of his inactions. Not by micromanaging Norman but by finding teachable moments as Norman grows in his newfound role. The team around Norman is also a fundamentally crucial part of his successful development, not only through their guidance in battle but their attitude as a whole. I couldn't imagine a worse situation to be in—hungry, hurt, tired, homesick—but every time they finish a battle, they laugh with each other and say, "This is best job in the world."

Some may say those guys are crazy, and maybe they are, but that is the culture we need to continue to create. No matter how hard the "battle" is, we are a team and this is the best job ever. When one person falls down, we pick up the slack. Their competence as a team makes Norman want to be a better gunner. If you are surrounded by talent, you will feel increasing pressure to step up your game to their level. Attitude and pace have to start with the leader.

Throughout the movie, the leader showed a great deal of trust in everyone aboard the tank and empowered them to handle their roles efficiently. The leader even trusted the new guy, Norman, to do what he was supposed to do. The leader would provide feedback, and Norman would improve. This is much easier said than done, but the leader handled this flawlessly. He would call out a direction for the tank to shoot and would trust his gunner to hit the target. In turn, his crew would trust him, wholeheartedly, even if they disagreed on his combat strategy. Trust is critical for a fully functional team. In times of war, there is no room for error and we must be able to trust everyone we work with to accomplish their tasks. With empowerment comes trust.

Let's not forget the generals. You could argue that if the Fury crew was not getting the best insight and direction, they would have been killed in battle—despite all the other positives they had as a team—and you would probably be right. Just as the crew followed the leader's vision for day-to-day combat, the leader followed the generals' decisions on wartime strategy. The leader understood that his value was rooted in his ability to lead a team into battle and that he didn't have the data necessary to make holistic strategic decisions.

In closing, the leader understood when to lead and when to follow. He knew when to take instruction and when to give it. He trusted the generals' strategic vision, and in turn, the leader's crew trusted his combat vision. It all starts with an excellent direction from the generals and ensuring there are competent leaders in place to follow that direction. The leaders must give their crews a reason to follow and to trust. Be the first one to stick your head out of the tank when there is heavy fire. Hold your ground when everyone else wants to run. Let's continue to create a squad of Furies.

I show you this old e-mail to say that you will have all the makings of a great leader one day. You have to learn to trust, empower and respect people, and they will follow you anywhere. Set a good example for them to follow. Be Christlike and honest in your approach to every problem you will face, even if it means giving up worldly success. You will be rewarded for it for all of eternity.

It took me a while to fully trust my team, but I always showed them respect and encouraged them to make mistakes. That is the only way to learn—to make and correct mistakes. I spent countless hours teaching myself how to code and made one million mistakes along the way. But I stuck with it, and it made me more valuable to Bellhops.

Pat Metheny, the jazz musician I mentioned earlier, first made his mark in 1974 when he began teaching at the prestigious Berklee College of Music at age nineteen. Twenty-two years later, he came back to give the 1996 commencement address to the students and faculty at Berklee. He said,

> For as much as I can stand here and claim to be a successful player, with Grammy awards and winning

polls and now honorary degrees and all that stuff; one very fundamental thing has not changed, and I realized that it will never change, and that is this: that the main thing in my life, even as I stand here right now, right this second, is that I really need to go home and practice.

And this is the most important part to me:

We all need to practice and improve. But I do think that when I was younger, I thought there would be a day when I would sort of "get it," and that everything would be cool, and I would have arrived at that promised land of being a great musician and I would just be. And I can see now that that is never going to happen.

He was, of course, speaking to young musicians about what it takes to be a great musician, but the wisdom in Pat Metheny's personal philosophy is highly relevant to our own lives and careers. He isn't in it for the fame, and almost certainly he never counts the trophies on his mantle. Rather, he is a musician because he loves music, and his complete dedication to practice is how he demonstrates that love and respect. The nature of practice is to find and correct mistakes.

I love what Elon Musk says about this.

Failure is an option here. If things are not failing, you are not innovating enough.

If you're not driven, if you're not willing to change and grow and correct your mistakes, then you will suffer the consequences. You have to practice. If, like Pat Metheny or the Berklee students, you want to play music, you have to lock yourself in the room and play the scales. If you're a founder trying to start a company, you have to practice all the skills relevant to your business.

In Daniel Coyle's book, *The Talent Code*, he talks a good deal about practice. Specifically, he says if you're not making mistakes while you are practicing, you will never reach your ultimate potential because you aren't willing to push the limits of what you are capable of doing.

Like Pat Metheny says, the day is never going to come when you just "get it." Think about how you can make yourself a better leader, for whatever your career path you choose, and constantly try to improve.

Everything seemed to be going so well. I was becoming the definition of a great leader, but at what cost? That is when God decided to step in and take the reigns.

The Diagnosis

Faithless is he that says farewell
when the road darkens.
—J. R. R. Tolkien, *The Fellowship of the Ring*

On June 4, 2015, we moved into our posh, new office space. After raising our series A, we had some breathing room for the first time in the company's history. So we decided it was time for us to move from the venture incubator and into our own space. Especially since our head count was around one hundred.

I was standing up to take my team out for a celebratory lunch when I started spinning and collapsed.

I woke up with a breathing tube shoved down my throat and had no idea why I was in a hospital. I saw a nurse and was able to scribble down, "What happened?" on a piece of paper. She told me I had three grand mal seizures. I was extremely confused. Why would I, an active and healthy twenty-eight-year old, have three seizures?

So once again, in my scrawled handwriting, I wrote, "Why the seizures?" The nurse said I had a mass the size of a baseball in my brain. *No way,* I thought. This couldn't be happening to me. There was a surely a mistake on the scan—a scan I wasn't even conscious for. I didn't believe it.

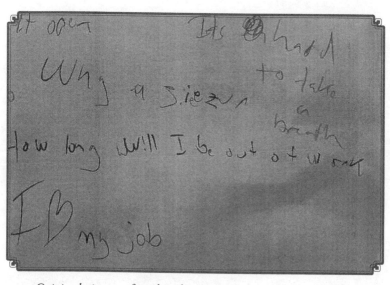

Original picture of my handwriting after initially waking up.

They took the breathing tube out of my throat, and I realized the gravity of the situation when, one by one, friends, family, and coworkers (you can just go ahead and lump them into the friends category) were all coming in to see me during the hospital's visiting hours.

I ended up taking an ambulance from Chattanooga to Knoxville's UT Medical Center, where we have a family friend who is a neurologist. He took a look at the scan and said it looked like it was fast growing, cancerous, and needed to come out immediately.

It was like time stopped. We immediately started researching surgeons, and after some deliberation, we found an incredible one: Dr. Reid Thompson at Vanderbilt University Medical Center in Nashville.

After meeting with him, I knew he was our surgeon. It wasn't about the number of tumors he has taken out (though that did play a factor); it was simply because I could see he truly cared about my family and me. He was passionate about his job and was ready for the tumor to come out, almost as ready as I was. He even scheduled the surgery on a day not usually set aside for surgeries.

Two weeks later, on June 19, 2015, Dr. Thompson resected 95 percent of the tumor. There are always microscopic tumor cells left behind, which is what the radiation and chemo attempt to destroy. The tumor was pressed up against my language and fine motor skills, so Dr. Thompson warned my family after the surgery that I may not be able to speak initially and would more than likely have to go to physical therapy for a period of time to get the right side of body working again—the tumor was on my left frontal lobe, thus controlling the right side of my body.

The first thing I remember after the surgery is that I reached up with my right hand, which wasn't supposed to be working at that point, and asked for some water, when I wasn't supposed to be speaking. Everyone was shocked, especially my family. I ended up walking out of Vanderbilt's neuro-ICU after three days.

You grandmother and grandfather on your mom's side—you call them Meepsie and B, kept you while we went back to Knoxville to Pops and Gimmi's house to rest after the surgery.

Meepsie and B have been incredible. I am sure you know by now, but they love you so much. I don't really talk about them enough since this book is about getting to know me, but they have been a big part of my life. They kept you during all my doctors' appointments, my recovery, and various times your mom and I just needed a break. They were a constant rock of stability through this time and have been angels to your mom and me.

I actually lived with Meepsie and B for about six months when I first moved to Chattanooga, while I was working at the bank. They had a pool table, and I remember playing game after game while B played southern rock, jazz, or whatever he had in the CD tray, at full blast. Those were incredible memories I will cherish forever.

Being the competitive person I am, I always made sure to keep a running tally of the games I won. They welcomed me with open arms in those six months and loved me like I was a son, and they continue to do so today. They have been the best parents-in-law I could ask for. Just know you will always be taken care of by your Meepsie and B.

Meepsie, you, me, and B after a 10K trail race.

They don't give a specific diagnosis right after the surgery, but they give you a quick pathology report. Dr. Thompson told us that it was fast growing but couldn't give us a full diagnosis.

It turns out we wouldn't get the full pathology report until a week later. We were all on pins and needles waiting for the call. We all thought it was a grade 3 on a scale of 1–4, which would give me a better prognosis.

The call came in from Dr. Thompson, and our whole family was there on speaker. It wasn't what we wanted to hear.

"I am sorry to tell you all, but it is grade 4, glioblastoma," Dr. Thompson said.

I completely tuned out after that. I am sure he talked for a good two minutes, but that's all I heard.

At this point, I knew what that meant. Statistically, I had fifteen months to live. Throw in being young and neurologically well after the surgery and chalk it up to twenty-four months. I was about to start the fight of my life, and I couldn't do it alone. Your mom is an amazing caregiver. I don't know how she manages all of my appointments and makes sure you get three square meals. I truly don't know where I would be without her. But this was bigger than her, and me, and I needed help from above.

Beginning to Trust

All we have to decide is what to do
with the time that is given us.
—J. R. R. Tolkien, *The Fellowship of the Ring*

I was struggling in every way imaginable. My thought process slowed, I wasn't as quick on my feet, I was becoming more forgetful, and I started realizing how much emphasis I placed on work and not my family. I was appalled at where my priorities had been. How could I have been this lost when things seemed so great?

Outwardly, most people would have wanted our lives. I was the VP of operations at a growing startup and your mom was the associate director of volunteer services, doing what she loved, but I was so caught up in how the world perceived us that I lost sight of what was important in life.

A blog by Jordan Nations wraps up what I am trying to say perfectly.

> You want to know God's plan? Here it is. Love
> God, love other people, make disciples. (Luke 10:27,
> Matthew 28:19) Really, that's it. He's already told us
> the plan through his Word, there's no need to search
> for his will anymore.

Your mom and I both were beyond blessed to have the jobs we had, but I know I failed at the most critical elements. I wasn't loving God, I mainly loved myself, and sure, I was respected at work and was well liked among the Bellhops family, but I definitely wasn't making any disciples.

I called myself a Christian, but was I really acting like one? I had no relationship at all with God, which is the foundation of Christianity. I was so broken spiritually that I didn't even know who or what I had become.

When a reputable doctor tells you that you have twenty-four months to live, I don't care who you are; your back will be against the wall and the only way to look is up. This is why I say it is the best worst thing that has happened to me, because it is the point where I had to start relying on God alone.

I always thought I was a trusting person until I had to trust people to do things for me. I am not sure if it was a pride/control thing or what, but when it came down to it, I was not okay with concept of trust. For example, my first night out of the hospital, I questioned every pill your mom gave me. "Are you sure I am supposed to take four of these? How many times a day? Are you sure?" I was convinced she was wrong about the dosage, including how many times a day to take them, but of course, she wasn't.

I have really learned to trust others and not rely on my own assessment of things.

Death isn't something I ever dwelled on, and now it consumed my every thought. My whole perspective on life changed at that moment.

Your mom and I began a true relationship with God. We started yearning for His love and grace and dove into the Word like we never had before. We put all our trust in Him and continue to do so today. We actually learned what Sunday school had been trying to teach us all along, which is that God is a loving God and nothing surprises Him.

Pops had a great analogy of this. He said,

> When we get to heaven, God will press a play button on our lives, and we will get to see our lives, the ripples of all our actions, and the ways we have impacted others. We can't have His perspective, because we couldn't begin to understand it.

To give an example, there was a young girl in medical school who watched Dr. Thompson perform my surgery. Dr. Thompson was so excited to tell me after the surgery that she completely changed course with her medical career, and due to watching how beautiful my surgery was, she wanted to become a neurosurgeon now. I always wanted to be a doctor growing up, so this was very special for me, but who knows how God will use this young woman who completely changed course to become a neurosurgeon? She may come up with a cure for this terrible disease or be the next Dr. Thompson.

The point is we don't have God's perspective, and we have to trust He knows what He is doing. He will use the pain and suffering in our lives to not only mold us to become more like Him but also for outcomes we can't even begin to imagine, like the young woman becoming a neurosurgeon.

9

Going Keto

> The objective, when you have cancer and
> want to combat fatality, is to make sure you
> find yourself in the long tail of the curve.
> —David Servan-Schreiber,
> *Anticancer, a New Way of Life*

I wanted to learn all about this disease I was diagnosed with, and what I could do to help prolong my time on earth, so I could spend as much time as possible with you and Mom. Work had become a distant fourth on the list.

Every book I read on cancer talked about the typical American diet being the cause of many types of cancer. I always associated diets with losing weight. Due to great genes and constantly being active, I could eat whatever I wanted to and couldn't gain a pound. Come to think of it, I never looked at a nutrition label until my diagnosis.

That is when I realized that diet is more than just a tool for people to lose weight. It is part of a healthy lifestyle, and I believe the most crucial part. As it is said in 1 Corinthians 6:19–20,

> Do you not know that your bodies are temples of the Holy Spirit, who is in you, whom you have received from God? You are not your own; you were bought at a price. Therefore honor God with your bodies.

Jack, you will deal with this, since you have skinny and active genes imbedded in your DNA from your mom and me. We already have to chase you around everywhere you go, and you are only two! I hope by the time you read this that all the fast food restaurants are gone or at least serving healthier options, which you should always get.

I really, *really* want to emphasize for you a good, balanced diet full of veggies, fruit, and a small helping of protein, instead of the typical American diet in which the meat is the main course and you have a starchy vegetable (like a baked potato) and a small portion of canned vegetables.

After my diagnosis, I completely switched up my diet and initially cut out all processed foods and sugar and added more salads and green vegetables. Then a good family friend had me look into the ketogenic diet. I initially said thanks, but no thanks, because there was so much change already happening in my life I couldn't bear to add any more.

I started reading medical journal articles—a lot of them. I watched a video of Dr. Thomas Seyfried specifically about how the ketogenic diet beats out chemotherapy in brain cancer. I decided to revisit the idea and dove straight in.

In a nutshell, cancer cells, especially in the brain, can only use glucose (sugar) for fuel. The tumor cells grow so quickly that they have a deficient mitochondria and can't use fat as an energy source. The keto diet tries to eliminate sugar as a fuel source and have the body solely rely on fat as fuel. The diet consists of 75 percent fat (good sources of fat include all kinds of nuts, avocados, coconut oil, vegan butter, etc.), 15 percent protein (salmon is always a good choice, and if you eat chicken, get the dark meat because it has the most fat content), and 10 percent carbs.

There was a June 5 devotional in *Streams in the Desert*, by L. B. Cowman, that really spoke to me, because I was struggling on how to pray for this disease. Do I ask for a miracle? What if that is not in His ultimate plan? Can I still attempt to prolong my life here on earth to spend quality time with my family? This daily devotional helped me answer these questions.

> We must keep on praying and waiting upon the Lord, until the sound of a mighty rain is heard. There is no reason why we should not ask for large things; and without doubt we shall get large things if we ask in faith, and have the courage to wait with patient perseverance upon Him, meantime doing those things, which lie within our power to do.
>
> We cannot create the wind or set it in motion, but we can set our sails to catch it when it comes; we cannot make the electricity, but we can stretch the wire along

upon which it is to run and do its work; we cannot, in a word, control the Spirit, but we can so place ourselves before the Lord, and so do the things He has bidden us do, that we will come under the influence and power of His mighty breath.

I knew the ketogenic diet would hopefully prolong my earthly life a little longer—setting my sails to catch the wind—but I knew I had no control of my life and had to trust in God.

Learning Humility

When pride comes, then comes disgrace,
but with humility comes wisdom.
—Proverbs 11:2

As soon as I received my diagnosis, a friend and fellow Bellhop named Adam Shearer started a youcaring.com page. Within two weeks, we raised $70,000 toward my medical bills, hotels, and all the extra stuff that comes with hospital visits.

Uncle Moo Cow has a T-shirt company, called TN Fly Co., that made shirts for me and all the proceeds from the sale of those shirts went to our family. My good friends Paul Dickenson and Blair Webber made "Fight Like Nate" bracelets and sold them for five dollars apiece, again, with all proceeds going to our family. The Bellhops family committed to paying me my salary for the next couple of years, whether I was at work or not.

We were blown away by the love and support shown by our extended family, the Bellhops family, and generous friends.

Bellhops even put together a sixteen-team home run derby, called Homers 4 Heroes, in my benefit. Really, the whole community rallied around me like I was one of their own.

I'll share some pictures from the event.

Mussy, me, Mom, you, and Aunt Hannah.

Pops and me.

You, Gimmi, and Pops.

There is this perceived weakness in accepting help, which was one of the first lessons that your mom and I had to learn. It's crazy to say, but it is really hard accepting money you did not earn. You have to relinquish your pride. I love the quote in C. S. Lewis' book, *Mere Christianity,* where he talks about pride being the greatest of all sins.

> How is it that people who are quite obviously eaten
> up with Pride can say they believe in God and appear
> to themselves very religious? I am afraid it means they
> are worshipping an imaginary God.

C. S. Lewis goes on to say that the opposite of pride is humility. We have to humble ourselves before Christ and realize we are not in control of our own lives. This is what your mom and I had to learn. Humility. For your mom and me, it was a hard process of accepting help, whether it was money, letters, or prayer, without reciprocating. It felt unnatural to us because we had never been in a position where we had to ask for help.

As it is said in Peter 5:5,

> All of you, clothe yourselves with humility toward one
> another, because, "God opposes the proud but shows
> favor to the humble."

We learned about humility in a big way by being able to accept these unreal gifts.

My team at Bellhops jumped in and took the reigns while I was out for surgery and the recovery, built onto my Lego towers, and by the time I was ready to start working half days, I didn't have anything to do! That's how amazing my team was and still is.

As I started working half days, I embarked on six months of radiation and concurrent chemotherapy. I would have a month off all treatment to let my brain heal from the radiation. During my month off, we were able to take a much-needed vacation to the beach. Once I returned, I would have to start monthly chemo cycles (five days on chemo and twenty-three days off) at triple the dose I had while I was doing radiation.

I was bummed, but through all this, I was trying to stay active, as I have always been. By the time I finished radiation in September, I was running a mile or two, which was a huge improvement from when I initially got out of surgery and could barely walk the half-mile lap around Pops and Gimmi's neighborhood without being completely winded.

I was back in the office for one of my half days when Adam Shearer started talking about running a half marathon that upcoming March. At that time, it was the first week of November 2015, and my second round of chemotherapy was about to begin. I, being the determined person I am, said, "Hey, I'll run it!" without regard to all the training involved. The most I had ever run in my life was seven miles. Remember? I was a sprinter and hated pain during long periods of time.

On November 7, 2015, with two weeks until I could drive again (Tennessee has a state law that you can't drive for six months after a seizure), I had another seizure. That meant I was stripped of driving privileges for another six months. Your mom, being the saint she is, had to drive me around for another six months. Not being able to drive also meant I had to do all my training where we lived in Signal Mountain, Tennessee. As you have probably realized by now, Signal Mountain is very, very hilly, and going downhill is what hurt my knee so bad. If running in flat Conway was bad, I was in a world of trouble trying to train for this half marathon.

There was a lot of pain ahead with more rounds of chemo coming, so I thought I would view this race as a metaphor: to suffer for a long period of time. Isn't that how God molds and shapes us? A grape vine that doesn't suffer through a drought will not have roots that grow deep enough to reap a good harvest the next year. Just like a grape vine, I needed to suffer to find my way to Him.

Pain and Suffering

We move forward, but we must
stay in the present.
—Scott Jurek, *Eat and Run: My Unlikely
Journey to Ultramarathon Greatness*

Due to your mom having to drive me around to doctors'
appointments, work, and all the other errands she had to squeeze
into her "free time," it made me really sad to see your mom quit
a job she loved in December 2015 to take care of me. Jack, you
have an incredible mom who has been put through the wringer
and come out more beautiful on the other side. Please listen to her
because I might not be around to tell you to do so.

As I prepared for the upcoming half marathon, with the
same hardworking DNA that is living in your veins, I started
out running five to ten miles a week and slowly working my way
up to around twenty miles a week. Hey! I was doing pretty well.
Then the inevitable IT band issue I had in my knee (commonly

called runner's knee) reared its ugly head around January. With only two months left until the race, I continued to try to run on it, but that just made it worse. With the knee issue in full swing and going through maintenance rounds of chemo, I was losing ground on my training plan fast.

I finally sought help from a podiatrist, and he recommended I have a custom orthotic made. I received my orthotic in February 2016, and back to training I went. I had a lot of training to make up for. My knee felt better but still was not great. What runner doesn't have knee problems? I would find out after I ran the half marathon that there were runners who could run more than one hundred miles a day without injury. I will get to that later on.

My last training run before the race was eleven miles on Signal Mountain at an 8:15 per mile pace. Given the flat nature of the half marathon course, I was shooting for an 8:00 per mile pace. If I was really lucky, I would go lower.

The Chattanooga *Times Free Press* wrote an article about the upcoming marathon and wanted to do a human story piece on me. I wanted to get my voice out in public for others fighting cancer or other life threatening diseases, to let them know to live each day to the fullest. Even with this horrible diagnosis I have, I can still enjoy life until the end and live in the present.

I actually had a verse (Matthew 6:34) inscribed on a ring that I gave your mom for Christmas, after all this happened. It says,

> Therefore do not worry about tomorrow, for tomorrow will worry about itself. Each day has enough trouble of its own.

The article came out on the Thursday before the race on Sunday. Through social media, the article found its way to a production company based out of Chattanooga. It is called Fancy Rhino. Drew Belz and Isaiah Smallman, the founders of Fancy Rhino, said after they read it, it brought the office to a standstill. They had the idea of doing a short documentary on my story.

Drew immediately called me on Thursday afternoon, and by Thursday evening, he was interviewing me at the Fancy Rhino headquarters, and we were out shooting a sunrise training run on Friday morning. This may be outdated by the time you read this, but I felt like I was a Kardashian with cameras following me everywhere. Let's just say I wouldn't have been a good famous person.

I am sure Mom will show you the video if you haven't seen it by now. They did an amazing job capturing the essence of my story, which to sum it up is "Love God, love other people, and make disciples."

I finished my first ever half marathon in 1:41:07, which breaks down into an average pace of 7:44 per mile. I learned valuable lessons about how to overcome pain and suffering through the whole training process and especially the race. God proved to me, during the race, that He had given me the focus and perseverance necessary to endure pain over long periods of time. Like a muscle having to be broken down before it gets stronger, God was using the pain of running as my unique way of finding Him.

You, Mom, and me. I'm trying not to fall
over after my first half marathon!

I have realized at a young age that there is beauty in suffering. I love this excerpt from Os Hillman's book *Upside to Adversity*. It has really stuck with me and taught me God is using whatever suffering we are going through in our lives to become more like Him.

> Someone once described suffering as God's manure for spiritual growth. Manure is not the most pleasant substance in the world, but we can't deny that it promotes growth.
>
> No matter what happens in our lives, we know that nothing happens without God's foreknowledge and permission. He always knows what we are going through—and why. God has a plan for the "manure" of our affliction. It is not a plan to hurt us, but to heal us and help us grow.

Everyone is going through some sort of suffering in their life, such as an illness, a broken relationship, unexpectedly becoming a caregiver, or money problems. It is all relative to that specific person, and they have a choice of how to deal with it.

Mussy steered me toward a book written by Viktor Frankl, a holocaust survivor, called *Man's Search for Meaning*, that discusses how we handle suffering. Suffering in and of itself is meaningless. We give our suffering meaning by the way we respond to it.

Let me explain using a great example from Frankl's book to help explain this concept. In his book, Frankl discusses his time in a concentration camp and how he made it out alive. Frankl describes a man who he is in Auschwitz with. This man is the essence of worldly success. He has a great job, multiple degrees, and respect from his peers. The Nazis then take him to a concentration camp, where he is stripped of everything: his dignity, job, degrees, and everything else that he has worked his entire life for. This man, whose self-esteem had been so wrapped up in worldly possessions, would go on to die. He would no longer be able to get back to the social class that he was in before he became a prisoner. In short he was humiliated. It was how he handled the suffering that killed him, not the lack of food or lack of medicine.

Frankl argues that we are never left with nothing as long as we retain the freedom to choose how we respond to adversity. In the example above, the man chose to respond by essentially rolling over and losing hope. He put all his weight and hope in how the world perceived him, and once that was gone, it killed him.

I love this quote:

> We have come to know man as he really is. After all, man is that being who invented the gas chambers of Auschwitz; however, he is also that being who entered those gas chambers upright, with the Lord's Prayer or the Shema Yisrael on his lips.
>
> —Harold S. Kushner

So what does this mean? If we put our hope in God and trust that He has a reason for our suffering, we will survive—maybe not on earth but where God has gone before us and prepared a room in heaven to spend eternity in. If we truly believe in eternal life, then why do we put so much stock in this life? Remove work or financial security from your life. Who are you now?

It's like a being young NBA prospect who has a great high-school career. Everyone is his "best friend," until he doesn't make the NBA. His identity is going to be so wrapped up in being the next Michael Jordan that he fails to see the big picture. Everyone who was his "friend" has now vanished. If he doesn't have that relationship with the Lord, he is going to fail to see there is a life away from this one—a life that is better. And if he could see how God is going to use his failure to make it to the NBA to mold him to be more Christlike, he would want it to happen too.

To sum it all up, what Frankl is trying to say is putting our hope in our eternal future is something no one can strip away from us.

The Tarahumara

Let us run with endurance the
race God has set before us.
—Hebrews 12:1 (NLT)

I wanted to run more, but I couldn't seem to get past this knee issue I had. A friend of mine recommended I read the book *Born to Run* by Christopher McDougall. I secretly thought, *How can reading a book help my knee problem?* but I read it based on his recommendation.

Jack, if there is only one book you ever read (well, besides the Bible), it needs to be *Born to Run*. Whether you end up being a runner or not, it is a must read. Chris McDougall hears about a tribe called the Tarahumara that lives in the Copper Canyons of Mexico, and its members can supposedly run more than one hundred miles a day without injury. To make things even more unrealistic, they would run in sandals! McDougall sets off to see if these people actually exist. To make a long story short, he finds them.

They are a quiet people but can run like the wind. They take quick, efficient strides and land on their forefeet—as opposed to heels striking first.

Shouldn't Americans, with their state-of-the-art shoe technology, be the ones leading the way in injury prevention? In fact, we aren't. When Nike introduced its first shoe in 1971, running injuries started becoming more frequent. Dr. Bernard Marti published a paper in which he surveyed 4,358 runners who participated in a sixteen-kilometer race and found that runners who ran in shoes costing more than ninety-five dollars actually were twice as likely to get injured as runners who ran in shoes costing only forty dollars. *What?*

The reason is one quarter of the bones in our bodies are in our feet. Also, there are thirty-three joints and more than one hundred muscles, tendons, and ligaments. In today's world, with all of this fancy support technology, we are preventing our feet from doing their main job: to stabilize the body. This puts the job of trying to stabilize the body on the knees and hips, which they are not meant to do.

So what do you do with all this information? If you end up being a runner (I swear I'm not trying sway your decision to be a runner), I would recommend buying some minimalist, barefoot-feel shoes to practice your forefoot strike and get your stride rate up. There is no way you can heel-strike in barefoot shoes, because you will be in a world of pain if you let your heel hit first. Start off running a half a mile, or a mile, and work your way up. Your calves will be in a lot of pain for the first month or two. Running in barefoot shoes isn't going to solve all your problems, but it will help a lot. Watch some YouTube videos on form, or read *The Cool Impossible* by Eric Orton.

Once you get your form down, you can start running in basic racing flats, which is what I have done for the past three months. I am running more miles and running faster than ever. The best part is I can run without pain in my knee.

I also learned something unexpected from *Born to Run*. I learned about the ways of the Tarahumara and how they treat each other. This little, poor tribe could have all the sponsorship money that the sport has to offer, if they chose to run in the big ultramarathon races—anything over marathon distance.

In the book, they race against one of the world's best ultramarathoners—Scott Jurek—and beat him. But they don't run in the big races. Instead, they live in little caves in Copper Canyon and choose to be like ghosts. Why? Because they just love to run. They don't want the attention or sponsorship money. They live quiet lives and depend on their community for survival. "What's mine is also yours" is their mentality. It's ingrained into their being. If I have excess corn, it is also yours. If I have extra chia seeds, you take them.

What an amazing thing to read about people that still exist in this day and age when self-centeredness is all around us. They are so selfless, when we are so selfish. The way the Tarahumara live is more Christlike than we will probably ever live. Philippians 2:3–4 (NASB) says,

> Do nothing from selfishness or empty conceit, but
> with humility of mind, regard one another as more
> important than yourselves; do not merely look out for
> your own personal interests, but also for the interest
> of others.

Much like the Tarahumara tribe, the community around the area has been incredible to us. The prayers, donations, and kind letters our family have received all mean so much.

13

Friendship

> Friendship is the least biological,
> organic, instinctive, gregarious, and
> necessary … the least natural of loves.
> —C. S. Lewis, *The Four Loves*

When I was in middle school, I got really into *The Lord of the Rings*. You could say I was obsessed. What is interesting in the books (not the movies) is that the whole story is about friendship. In the books, you have to look in the appendixes to find the love story of Aragorn and Arwen, but in order to sell out box offices, you have to put the love story front and center.

Friendship is the only deliberate kind of love. Think about it. When work gets busy, what is the first thing to drop off this list? Certainly not your spouse or other relatives because they are dependent on you to bring food home. Love for a sibling is also born out of a sense of loyalty. Your friends are the first to drop off the list.

In a 2005 sermon Tim Keller gives on friendship, he says, "You will not lead a wise life unless you are great at choosing, forging and keeping terrific friendships." A friendship is first built on a common interest. Whether that is sports, work, shared academic interests, etc., once a friendship is built, you are not done there. He goes on to discuss what he calls the four c's of a lasting friendship.

Constancy

A friend loves at all times. You have to be there when the chips are down. Most of the people you call friends are useful to you. Either they have an ulterior motive for being your friend or you have a reason for being their friend.

I had a talk with a friend recently who is still in the financial advising world, and he hates that he has to pretend to like certain wealthy people. Even if their moral compasses are off, he has to put on a smiling face every time they are around. After my short stint in the financial advising world, I totally get it. It is hard to have true friends in that world—friends who will be there when it all comes crashing down.

Carefulness

You have to be emotionally vulnerable to be a good friend. You have to be able to share and connect with your friends at tough points in their lives. What is painful for them must also be painful for you. This plays into the next C.

Candor

Be honest with each other. It's selfish to not want to put through someone through pain, because it will also put you in pain. If one of your true friends is an addict, it is going to be hard to tell them the truth, because it is going to be just as painful for you.

Wes Bailey—I am assuming by the time you read this he will be a rock star—is one of my best friends. When your mom and I—before we got married—were going through a tough time, he wrote me an e-mail I will never forget. It was painful to hear, because it was when your mom and I were broken up. He was telling me that a girl like your mom comes around once in a lifetime. If I didn't see that, I was an idiot. It was the essence of candor. The thing is I could tell it was just as painful for him to write it as it was for me to read it. Next time you see him, tell your uncle Wes thanks for being candid with me at a time when I needed it most.

Counsel

As iron sharpens iron, you sharpen one another. You can never become the person you can be without a friend's strong counsel.

I can think of countless examples of this, but one really sticks in my mind. A family friend, Billy Blount, who is about Pops's age, came down to the beach with us this past year. We had a difficult, but great, conversation about death and heaven. He went on to tell me story after story of different dreams and experiences he had had regarding heaven. I was in tears by the time it was over because it was such a powerful conversation. In short, it was great counsel, at a much-needed time, by a great friend.

———————

Why did I go into all this depth about friendship? Since my diagnosis, there have been people who have been true friends, who I would expect would be there for me—the reliable ones.

But there are also new friends I have made through this. Truth be told, I don't think I would be as true of a friend as they have been to me if the tables were turned and they were the ones with a cancer diagnosis. These have been the most impactful friendships, because they were founded on a love for Christ and built upon by the four c's mentioned above.

We all need a few, if not more, of these true friendships in our lives.

A great example of a true friend is David Nichols—Grainger's dad. I knew David before my diagnosis, but we weren't great friends. I would say we were good acquaintances. I knew him as the rugged guy who loved to turkey hunt and saw him around at the gym I used to work out at. I am not much of a hunter, so we didn't really have much to talk about.

He would be in the category of people that, if the tables were turned and he was the one receiving the brain-tumor diagnosis, I don't think I would have been as good of a friend to him as he has been to me.

Through all of this, he has been the essence of constancy and a true friend. We built our foundation on Christ and built upon it with the four c's mentioned in the chapter above. We have had so many great conversations about God and pain and suffering that I can't even begin to count them.

David sent me an e-mail recently that I want to share with you.

> We all leave this earth. Most of us assume we will leave when we get old and it's our time to move on. Most of us assume that we will not be in a car accident, that we will not have an illness, or some other type of unplanned thing will happen that might make our departure from earth more premature than planned. Whether we live to be 100 or we live to be 20, this life is a glimpse. It's nothing. It's a quick fling where you have a brief opportunity to figure out what it's all about, where it came from, who the architect was.

> Life is a quick little blink, where we all try to find these answers in our own unique way. We all have a death date.

> We all leave. Most of us do not know when that will be, so most of us stroll through life taking it granted. You were never given a death sentence. You were given a life sentence. You were given an idea of what kind of time you might have left in your fling with this world. That is what is so beautiful about your situation to me. You are so alive now and so are so many others around you.

My "unique way" of sorting through this life has always been through the natural world. Mostly through hunting, I'd say. So that you understand, "hunting" means more to me than killing something. While that is the understood goal, a lot of people don't realize that an animal isn't what they are truly after. Hunting is an avenue for me to disappear—for me to melt and fade away and observe everything that doesn't know I am there—for me to appreciate not just my life but life in general.

One of the most important things I have learned is that nature is as brutal as it is beautiful, and the beauty is derived from the brutality. Every animal, every living being, benefits from the loss of another whether it's through nourishment or through a lesson learned in survival. Everything lives for each breath and no other creature or living thing on this earth takes one for granted—only us. When one goes, the others are forever changed in some way, and the life that death produces is even more beautiful than the one before it. We all have to wonder what we will leave behind and who will benefit from it, and how. We are not here for ourselves. We are here for each other. You have been here for me, and I am here for you. Your time is short and so is mine. I love you, buddy.

I have cherished the conversations David and I have had, and there is going to be a point in your life when you begin to choose the people you hang out with. I use the relationship David and I have forged over the past year as a great example of a friend who will be there when the chips are down.

I was talking to Mussy recently about friendships, and she said, "It's interesting that God puts friends in your life that bring out certain characteristics in you." I didn't really think much about it at the time, but now that I have had a chance to reflect on it, it is so true.

I can sit and reminisce on memories with old family friends like Michael Blount. I can't ever remember not being friends with Michael. Growing up, we did everything together. We share a deep connection, with a long history, that I can't share with my other friends. We can share old stories about our annual camping trips, which we have done since we were children, and always seem to pick up right where we left off. Michael is a once-in-a-lifetime friend.

Michael Blount and I are trying to catch dinner at the beach.

Travis Truett, Jared Houghton, and I used to go climbing together in college all the time. They bring out an adventurous side of me. I remember times with Jared fly fishing out on the Hiwassee River. He usually caught all the fish, but I would always snag a couple. Travis and I went to Europe together the summer after we graduated. We flew into Barcelona with our backpacks, a seven-day Eurail pass (which meant we had seven days to travel), our hammocks, and no plan. It was a trip I will always remember, but there is no way I could have done it without Travis by my side. We had so much fun slumming around the streets of Monaco, Rome, Chamonix, Nice, Paris, and many other cities. You will have to get him to tell you all about it sometime. It was a special trip.

Walter Sheppard, Wes Bailey, Blair Webber, Ryan Pate, and Chase Carroll—some of my friends from high school—bring out a fun side of me. I always have a good time when I am around them. They are the funniest group of people when we all get back together. They are your go-to people for dirt on me back in high school. I am sure they will have plenty of stories to share with you as you get older.

Friends like David Nichols, Paul Dickenson, Stephen Vlahos, Matt Patterson, Adam Shearer, and Cam Doody bring out a deep, sensitive side of me. I feel like I can open up to them at any point in time and they will listen. I have had a lot of great conversations where I have been at my worst and they have built me back up.

Use friendship to find the beauties of others and to see what good characteristics others can bring out in you. Friends are like fine wines. The vines grow deep in good soil and each element, whether it is the sun, soil, flowers, or the barrel it is aged in, brings out a different flavor. Each friend brings out a different "flavor" in you.

We live in a culture where, due to mobility and limited time, we do not have all the friends our hearts need because *we* are not good friends.

Be a good, true friend, because some of the best, most memorable times we have in our lives are with friends. Whether it's going on a run with a friend, going hunting with a friend, or just hanging out watching TV, enjoy the time you spend with them and forge solid friendships. Make time for them and be available when they call for help.

I will end the chapter with verses from John 15:12–13 and 17.

> This is my commandment, that you love one another as I have loved you. Greater love has no one than this, that someone lays down his life for his friends … These things I command you, so that you will love one another.

The Lord feels whatever pain you are feeling at the moment. He is with you every step of the way. He is the perfect friend.

Finding Your Way

Show me your ways, LORD, teach me
your paths. Guide me in your truth and
teach me, for you are God my Savior,
and my hope is in you all day long.
—Psalm 25:4–5

I have mentioned running a lot in this book. The reason is because through the pain and suffering of running I am able to feel His presence—when I am exerting myself to the limit of my capability. You may not be a runner, and I am totally okay with that! In David's e-mail to me, he finds his "unique way" of experiencing God through nature, by way of hunting.

Your "unique way" may be something completely different. Maybe you find it in your already apparent musical ability, but whatever it is, make sure you do it in a way that pleases God. Give it all you have and don't give up. Anything worth doing is worth doing well, and giving your best effort is what glorifies God.

Mistakes will be made along the way, and that is okay. Continue to persevere, and you will be rewarded.

Life can be painful, and I hope you are able to see the beauty of pain through my story. God will harness pain and use it for something good, even if you can't see the purpose in your suffering. Like I said earlier, nothing surprises God. He gave me this diagnosis and through it has given your mom and me the greatest gift we have ever received. He gave us life like we have never experienced it before—a life full of Him. And it doesn't end with that. He has provided me with incredible platforms through Bellhops, this book, blog posts, etc. to tell my story of God's love for us.

God goes before us in every way imaginable. He went before me in college, when your mom and I met. He knew I would need a strong, levelheaded wife to step into my battle with cancer, and she has done just that. I don't know where I would be without her. She has been my rock of stability through all of this. He went before me when I made the decision to switch jobs and take a 50 percent pay cut to work for a startup. Bellhops has been incredible to our family. They have allowed me to change roles, due to my circumstances, and were really the ones who encouraged me to start writing, since it is something I can do at my own pace.

You are already incredibly smart, and I hope you have the wisdom to take these lessons to heart. Learn from my successes, but even more so from my missteps. You have the perfect Father in heaven. Depend and lean on Him and His Word in times of need. It took me a while to learn this, but I finally found my relationship with Him.

Keep and cherish this book as a reminder that I will always love you. Do your best to remember our time on earth is like the blink of an eye—a single speck in time before we are reunited again.

I love you more than you can imagine,

Dad

You and I are playing superheroes!

Update

It has been eight months since I began this book, so you are getting close to your third birthday! I am so grateful for each day that God has given me to be with you, your mom, and our family as a whole. I have learned to cherish the days that pass and not take a moment for granted.

Once I finished the book, I was told that the tumor had progressed, which means the radiation and rounds of chemo did not work as we had hoped. This was kind of a double-edged sword, because we knew that glioblastoma almost always comes back—it is only a matter of time. God knows my personality and knows I am impatient. So in a sense, it was a gift to have the tumor come back earlier rather than later, because it opened up the door to clinical trials. That also meant I would be stopping chemotherapy, which I dreaded taking every month.

I was nervous but excited to enter the clinical trial world. Regardless of the outcome, I was helping doctors and scientists find a cure for brain cancer. Clinical trials exist for the sole purpose of attempting to find a cure, so you could see this as a possibly more curative approach than just prolonging my life by taking chemotherapy. We had our sights set on a phase 1 trial at Mayo Clinic in Rochester, Minnesota, which involved another surgery. They would be removing the tumor and injecting a modified measles virus in the tumor cavity in an attempt to stimulate the body's own immune system. Since the body knows to fight measles, the theory is it would know how to attack the tumor since the measles virus would be injected into the tumor.

I had our plane tickets ready and hotel room booked until we met with Dr. Thompson, the surgeon who performed my initial surgery. He told us another surgery would be a big risk. I read between the lines that he was urging us to not operate again. Dr. Thompson steered us toward Dr. Nabors at University of Alabama at Birmingham (UAB) and said they had some other immunotherapy drug trials that did not require surgery. Basically, immunotherapy treatments are just a way of getting your immune system revved up and ready to attack. Dr. Thompson made a great point: I have been given incredible quality of life, considering my situation. Why go through giving up the things you love to embark on a risky surgery? Another surgery would mean another month and a half of recovery, which would mean being away from you, Mom, and all of our family. I am also in the best running shape I have ever been in, so I would have to start from scratch again. I canceled the hotels and flights, and we set off to see Dr. Nabors.

We set up a consultation with Dr. Nabors and loved him. UAB offered a couple of phase 1 (out of four phases, with the fourth one being FDA approval) immunotherapy drug trials for recurrent glioblastoma. Without going into the details of the drugs, we chose the trial we thought sounded most promising, and my team of doctors and nurses at UAB couldn't be more amazing.

I am now going down to Birmingham, Alabama, every two weeks for a drug infusion that is supposed to stimulate my immune system. My most recent MRI showed the tumor as stable, which is great news and shows that the drug is working! All praise is to God!

God has given me the ability to continue to run, and with my new, improved form, I have been able to complete a bunch of different races with varying distances—a ten-mile trail race, a fifteen-kilometer trail race, a ten-kilometer trail race, an 8K, and a 5K. I have fallen in love with trail running because not only do you have to live in the present—since you constantly looking out for roots and rocks—but you get to see God's beauty that He has created through nature.

Pops, Gimmi, Aunt Hannah, Uncle Moo Cow, and your mom all went out to Napa Valley, California, which was a dream for your mom and me. Pops and I were able to run the Napa to Sonoma half marathon—my second half marathon, which I finished in 1:31:48—about ten minutes faster than my first half marathon! I have decided to hang up my road shoes and start solely doing ultramarathons, with my first one being a 50K here in Chattanooga called the StumpJump.

I am so thankful that God used Dr. Thompson (because I wouldn't have listened to anyone else since I am kind of stubborn—ha ha) to steer me away from that surgery. I am now able to enjoy each day to the fullest and maintain my quality of life until God decides to call me home.

References

All Scripture references are from the NIV translation of the Bible, unless otherwise noted.

Chapter 1 Growing Up

"God made me fast. And when I run, I feel His pleasure." Putnam, David (producer); Hudson, Hugh (director); Welland, Colin (writer), 1981. *Chariots of Fire*. United Kingdom. Warner Bros. and 20th Century Fox.

Chapter 2 Strengths and Weaknesses

"The ultimate measure of a man is not where he stands in moments of comfort and convenience, but where he stands at times of challenge and controversy." Martin Luther King Jr., BrainyQuote.

com. Xplore Inc., 2016. June 10, 2016. http://www.brainyquote.
com/quotes/quotes/m/martinluth109228.html.

Chapter 3 Meeting Your Mom

"Simplicity and complexity need each other." Maeda, John. *The Laws of Simplicity.* Cambridge, MA: MIT Press, 2006. Print.

Chapter 4 Passion for Work

"I used to be afraid of failing at something that really mattered to me, but now I'm more afraid of succeeding at things that don't matter." Goff, Bob. *Love Does: Discover a Secretly Incredible Life.* Nashville, TN. Thomas Nelson, 2012. Print.

"All work has dignity because it reflects God's image in us, and also because the material creation we are called to care for is good." Keller, Timothy. *Every Good Endeavor: Connecting Your Work to God's Work.* New York, New York. Penguin Group, 2012. Print.

Hsieh, Tony. *Delivering Happiness: A Path to Profits, Passion, and Purpose.* New York: Business Plus, 2010. Print.

Chapter 5 Growing a Company

"If you personally want to grow as fast as your company, you have to give away your job every couple months." Graham, Molly.

"Give Away Your Legos and Other Commandments for Startups."
http://firstround.com/review/give-away-your-legos-and-other-commandments-for-scaling-startups/. First Round Review,
September 10, 2015. Web.

Page x. Grove, Andrew S. *High Output Management*. New York:
Random House, 1983. Print.

Page x. "The best metaphor I have for scaling is building one
of those huge, complex towers out of Legos," she says. "At
first …" Graham, Molly. "Give Away Your Legos and Other
Commandments for Startups." http://firstround.com/review/give-away-your-legos-and-other-commandments-for-scaling-startups/.
First Round Review, September 10, 2015. Web.

Chapter 6 Becoming a Leader

"Best job I ever had." *Fury*. Director David Ayer. Performers Bill
Block, John Lesher, Alex Ott, Ethan Smith, Brad Pitt, and David
Ayer. Columbia Pictures, 2014. Film.

Metheny, Pat B. "Commencement 1996." Berklee College of
Music 1996 commencement address, Boston. June 1996. Speech.
< https://www.berklee.edu/commencement/past/1996>.

"Failure is an option here. If things are not failing, you are not
innovating enough." Musk, Elon, BrainyQuote.com. Xplore Inc.,
June 12, 2016. http://www.brainyquote.com/quotes/quotes/e/
elonmusk750652.html.

Coyle, Daniel. *The Talent Code: Greatness Isn't Born: It's Grown, Here's How*. New York: Bantam, 2009. Print.

Chapter 7 The Diagnosis

"Faithless is he that says farewell when the road darkens." Tolkien, J. R. R. *The Lord of the Rings: The Fellowship of the Ring*. London: HarperCollins, 2001. Print.

Chapter 8 Beginning to Trust

"All we have to decide is what to do with the time that is given us." Tolkien, J. R. R. *The Lord of the Rings: The Fellowship of the Ring*. London: HarperCollins, 2001. Print.

"You want to know God's plan? Here it is. Love God, love other people, make disciples. (Luke 10:27, Matthew 28:19) Really, that's it. He's already told us the plan through his Word, there's no need to search for his will anymore." "Quit Telling Me God Has a Plan." Nations, Jordan. April 12, 2016. Web. June 12, 2016. <https://jordannations.com/2016/04/12/quit-telling-me-god-has-a-plan/>.

Chapter 9 Going Keto

"The objective, when you have cancer and want to combat fatality, is to make sure you find yourself in the long tail of the curve."

Servan-Schreiber, David. *Anticancer: A New Way of Life*. New York: Viking, 2008. Print.

Seyfried, Thomas N., PhD. "Targeting Energy Metabolism in Brain Cancer." 2nd Annual Ancestral Health Symposium. Boston College Biology Dept., Boston. January 17, 2013. Lecture. <https://www.youtube.com/watch?v=sBjnWfT8HbQ>.

Cowman, Charles E., and James Reimann. "June 5th." *Streams in the Desert: 366 Daily Devotional Readings*. Grand Rapids, MI: Zondervan Pub. House, 1997. Print.

Chapter 10 Learning Humility

"How is it that people who are quite obviously eaten up with Pride can say they believe in God and appear to themselves very religious? I am afraid it means they are worshipping an imaginary God." Lewis, C. S. *Mere Christianity: A Revised and Amplified Edition, with a New Introduction, of the Three Books, Broadcast Talks, Christian Behaviour, and Beyond Personality*. San Francisco: HarperSanFrancisco, 2001. Print.

Chapter 11 Pain and Suffering

"We move forward, but we must stay in the present." Jurek, Scott, and Steve Friedman. *Eat & Run: My Unlikely Journey to Ultramarathon Greatness*. Boston: Houghton Mifflin Harcourt, 2012. Print.

Cobb, David. "With Months to Live, One Chattanooga Man Battles Cancer and This Weekend's Half Marathon." *Times Free Press*. Np, March 3, 2016. Web. June 16, 2016. <http://www.timesfreepress.com/news/local/story/2016/mar/03/taking-temodar-instead-tylenol-one-local-mpac/353136/>.

Fight Like Nate. Belz, Drew (director). Nelson, Katie (producer). Fancy Rhino and Mama Bear Productions, 2016. <https://www.youtube.com/watch?v=BHyJe1GQ3ns>.

"Someone once described suffering as God's manure for spiritual growth. Manure is not the most pleasant substance in the world, but we can't deny that it promotes growth. No matter what happens in our lives, we know that nothing happens without God's foreknowledge and permission. He always knows what we are going through-and why. God has a plan for the "manure" of our affliction. It is not a plan to hurt us, but to heal us and help us grow." Hillman, Os. *The Upside of Adversity*. Ventura, CA: Regal, 2006. Print.

Frankl, Viktor E. *Man's Search for Meaning*. Boston: Beacon, 2006. Print.

Chapter 12 The Tarahumara

Marti, B., J. P. Vader, C. E. Minder, and T. Abelin. "On the Epidemiology of Running Injuries: The 1984 Bern Grand-Prix

Study." *The American Journal of Sports Medicine* 16.3 (1988): 285–94. Web. <http://ajs.sagepub.com/content/16/3/285>.

Swierzewski, John J., DPM. "Foot & Ankle Anatomy." Foot Anatomy. Healthcommunities.com, December 30, 1999. Web. June 12, 2016. <http://www.healthcommunities.com/foot-anatomy/foot-anatomy-overview.shtml>.

Orton, Eric. *The Cool Impossible: The Coach from Born to Run Shows How to Get the Most from Your Miles and from Yourself.* 2013. Audible. Train With Eric LLC. Web. <http://www.audible.com/pd/Sports/The-Cool-Impossible-Audiobook/B00HHGEV8W>.

McDougall, Christopher. *Born to Run: A Hidden Tribe, Superathletes, and the Greatest Race the World Has Never Seen.* New York: Alfred A. Knopf, 2009. Print.

Chapter 13 Friendship

"Friendship is the least biological, organic, instinctive, gregarious, and necessary ... the least natural of loves." Lewis, C. S. *The Four Loves.* New York: Harcourt, Brace, 1960. Print.

Keller, Timothy. "Friendship." Redeemer Presbyterian Church sermon. Redeemer Presbyterian, New York. May 5, 2005. Speech.

41607717R00069

Made in the USA
San Bernardino, CA
16 November 2016